A DEDICATION TO INCOHERENCE

Denver Crawford

BookLeaf Publishing

India | USA | UK

A Dedication To Incoherence

© 2021 Denver Crawford

All rights reserved.

No part of this publication may be reproduced, stored in a retrieval system, or transmitted, in any form or by any means, electronic, mechanical, photocopying, recording or otherwise, without the prior written permission of the presenters.

Denver Crawford asserts the moral right to be identified as author of this work.

Presentation by *BookLeaf Publishing*

Web: www.bookleafpub.com

E-mail: info@bookleafpub.com

ISBN: 9789358738629

First edition 2021

"Nothing is more sad than the death of an illusion."

-Arthur Koestler

For My Lovers, Friends, And Enemies, For Covid-19, And

For Nothing Else.

1.

I've only just begun

   to care about corners,

  the cleaning of them

   their gravity for grime

   I mean I've just scraped

mold from my Brita filter,

  pitcher of life

   cold container that chills

   overnight in the fridge

I don't believe I'll keep it up.

sympathetic to a kind

of schizophrenia

  like endless prepositions

dust gathers

ink fades

love conquers

and death takes

my poems for a hundred friends

bleeding from

the corners

of my eyes

is your shoulder dry?

2.

Interior: unrepeating

memories behind my eyes

accumulating like dark matter;

      unfixed negatives

      I'm saving for

      double exposure.

Some things are for letting go.

I couldn't seem to list them

if you asked me.

There is some love I believe in

that keeps death waiting at the door.

The forward direction,

unappealing but

inevitable.

I'm letting go

of some kind of fear

that I'm anything but solid.

I can't articulate it here

and now, but soon

my meaning will appear.

3.

Spring cleaning

only done

because a dog

you met online

is coming home

to you and yours

forever. Home

is a cage made

comfortable

by any means

necessary.

The walls

singing

as I scrape

spores and all

manner of germs

from their

surfaces.

Time spent

remaking space

is as difficult

as exorcism.

New life

can only follow

death.

4.

Fuck the narrative.

They say

we design our own cages,

but I'd mince words

with the nonce

who wrote the story of the cave.

The ninety-nine philosophers

have nothing on the fool

making chaos out of chaos

and birthing laughter.

The space we skin

holds everything in.

I would break over

the glass desert

like golden fleece;

thread by thread.

    A thousand nothings

      for a farthing.

      Sex like death;

  big bang,

big bang.

5.

I am finished weeping

    for now.

I must try building

    something new.

I lack foundation

    like a plane

    put together

    mid-flight.

I hear the song

    of sinking sand

    echoing in my abandoned cathedral

    with the smells

    of oils, incense, and wood.

I make memory

    into new life

    to feed the aching spirit

    begging to be tethered.

I have removed

    the nails from my palms and feet,

    and I must heal

    before I find that hill

    where I will be raised,

    again, to shoulder

    darkness waiting.

6.

A reckless yes

before a quiet no.

I must now listen

to wounded cries of separation

and hold back my love

for the sake of the child.

Any place

can become a prison

for fear of certain

change.

A hundred locks

to hold

a hundred keys,

and freedom would still be

out of reach

held behind tears.

I lack the energy

to write today

but I won't let

words cage me.

7.

You are in front of me

solid, except the idea of you

expressed through my eyes

as a million points of data

how you sit

how you speak

every gesture, sound

and breath I gather

putting you together

piece by piece

into an idea

of someone I once knew

when things were new

just new information

adding to the pile

on my hard drive

heading toward capacity

8.

A day late

   and several dollars short

      I arrive

Nothing but the wind

   at my back

      and the sun on my face

Industry standards

   dictate the terms and conditions

      of the latest agreement

Selling sex

   seems the only currency

      in the information age

And the tower

  is still rising

    like a wave of brick and mortar

I would scream louder

  if only I believed

    I could be heard

But that's everyone

  nowadays

    afraid of being quiet

And me

  typing what

    I'm avoiding

9.

And we danced around your canvas

 talking to eternity

 helping you run away

  more easily

  from the mirror city

   And you worked with a magic

   I've only rediscovered

   in myself

   And I'm always telling you

   it will only ever be O.K.

   And I'm also saying it

   to remind myself

that time is a solid

and we are the wave of electricity

pulsing from the center

and moving toward the final edge

remaining undefined

But do not fear

as everything is

as everything will

be

10.

> The number death
>
> to weep again
>
> refusing me
>
> replacing him
>
> at the back of the bus
>
> on the walk to school
>
> Beckett danced in my ears
>
> but if I
>
> sure
>
> misplaced somehow
>
> bleeding from the organ
>
> the reeds hum anger
>
> in the woods
>
> behind the marsh
>
> Old Native American magic
>
> became him

and the earth

jumped to meet

the awaiting sky

11.

Cord uncut

    until the birth

    not mine

    but hers

        everything reminders

          but you the only

          rememberer

            sound first

             and then light

             sometimes neither

             self unknown

            except through others

lidless eyes

inside

bloodshot

pick up patterns

emerging from chaos

because gravity is irregular

still waiting

to cut

or perhaps rip

red thread

around my wrist

12.

I grew up

in the woods

behind my house

six feet above

sea level

I watched water

flood with every rain

fall

the simple melodies

of life where it's quiet

crescendo into violence

with repetition

change must come

for me at least

every new moon

    it's never long

after you've begun

that you remember

what you've forgotten

     go back and get it

there is no shame

in forgetting

     sankofa

13.

Lucky

you might call me

to avoid the responsibilities

of modern life

Timelessness

only results

from creation

A kind of carelessness

permeates my relationship

to language

Who am I today

Who will I be tomorrow

Who might I be to you

A stickbug dances

on a branch outside my window

It seems there are birds

looking for him

He dances

when they have flown

I sing

when no one listens

14.

If a tragedy

is not documented

is there any hope for justice?

Impossible to think

in terms of win or lose

I've become an armchair

philosopher more than poet

witness more than participant

And I've got hemorrhoids

bulging, sore and sensitive

bumps just around my

asshole

I debate

whether to share

or maintain some

artifice

But if I'm being read

might as well be honest

and share what's uncomfortable

15.

The faithless attempt of articulation

songs unheard

labor delayed

I will find distraction anywhere

Mercury like mirrors

the looking glass poison

hopelessly incoherent

and still searching for shape

Mother said to me "always be ready."

My felicitousness is grown

from a patience unknown to many

As I thrust off

the weight of "my generation"

I am free to join

the human race

It's no longer a question

of if

I keep it up

but how

I would learn to walk

when suddenly, again

I find myself

rebirthing

16.

The disintegration of time

        fading into the white noise

where tick-tocking becomes analogue

        and our circular clocks relicate

One begins to represent "whale"

        where baleen snags hashtags

as we swallow in a sea of information

        dwarfing even the biggest fish

Association no longer necessary

        except the most relevant meme

I struggle to place value

        on my cloud expression

Today, fluffy and dense

        tomorrow, electric and heavy

forming and falling

        rising and fading

The science-fiction nightmare

        sheering our domesticated fleece

to spin a new time fabric

        Kente cloth

Weavers and wearers

        unquestioning

the second skin

        become irremovable

17.

The whole system

shock and die

rigor mortis throughout the shell

echo in the dark

echo in the dark

come back from nothing

how do you come back from nothing

you don't come back from nothing

you are born with it

and give it form

you fill it with your time

you celestial body

you manna of the gods

you ancient words

of becoming

speak life

speak life

and bring her to me

in the morning

18.

I became poet

when ego left

writing songs

only in rhythm

you   can   surrender

to your circumstance

present in rooms

only   entered

never   left

you've never left

and when you do

rooms will ache

with   longing   like

shells' ocean   song

waves, breath, motion

mind becoming sound

the schizophrenia

a reminder of you

amongst expressions

of   the   same   beast

life   persisting

death reuniting

19.

Three days ago

I said aloud

                    "I don't want to die."

My therapist and I

talked termination

considering its implications

without actual articulation

No cure for life

just sustained behavior

like writing poems every day

I'm leaving room for harmony

in how I walk and talk

letting lyrics flow

My song

finally

my own

I just might try

singing joy

to the world

All I ask

is for patience

All I am

is for you

20.

Thread I tied in solidarity

red around my wrist

worn until Gaiya began to birth

untied itself exactly in time

Three days and nights

is long enough

for life to change

Duration a priority

for those concerned with living

Now, it is the budding leaves

fractal growth tapping at my window

that has only reached three stories high

with roots three stories down

Reaching skyward

where clouds wisped into cobweb oceans

hold back sunlight

from the atmosphere floor

I draw back the curtains

every morning

with a new love

I greet the day

with new comfort

Present at eternity's gate

21.

Someday I'll speak

in numbers

while articulation eats

its own tail

caught up in everywhere

but here

take a breath

to name yourself

window writer

distanced

thumping head

like typewriter mallets

free from everything

is bound to nothing

temporary walls

for temporary rooms

the only way out

demolition

the illusion of doors

kicked in

22.

Today

a change in weather

Just before

Spring swings full

Cold falling

on peeking blossoms

Inhale sharp

then pollen burst

Air pushes

through window screens

Sun bathes

your skin in honey

Another day

unfolds it's leaves

For you

to pollinate softly

Buzzing ink

page to page to page

23.

AN ATTEMPT AND MISS AT HONEST SOUND:

4 5

Nothing new under the sun

growth crawls from shadows

warm earth blanket waiting

for your eternal rest

Death feared and avoided

no longer

transitioning with every breath

Life twitching, ticking

in and out of wait

balance beating in the chest

come clarity

an idea cannot translate

instead forever searching

for an answer

questions dress

exhaustion only logical

machines become ornate

a slowly shuffle or recoil

leaves work always undone

24.

Repeated gestures on white

changing the same expression

to attempt peace with the nebulous

exercising some muscle

for more than one purpose

insanity more valid

out of context

placing perspective

becomes a habit

to be removed in private

past a certain fear of loneliness

failure becomes a kind of comfort

confusion coming from the outside

the struggle structures itself

and some days

you read yourself

and find nothing

25.

I'd like to place America

somewhere it could see itself

perhaps a mirror large enough

could show the land

its size, its expanse, its prolific nature

so abstract, it seems

America is more color than shape

more sound than space

and more comparison than metaphor

there are words

that have yet to meet each other

in a sentence

images unpainted or taken

is something new needed

or something more concrete?

by all known laws, I believe

that gravity forms slowly, imperceptibly

until a thousand years have passed

and future souls dig at the earth

to think about time lost

and to pretend the dirt

contains more answers than body

is ignorant of freedom

harmony is manifold

and holds all manner of death

and sound is different than sight

touch unlike taste

and smell, the mystery

some small way

to know what should be taken in

and what decay we must avoid

26.

Zoom room fatigue

is a phrase

I pray dates itself

My relationship to technology

having come too far

to lose to apocalypse

I walk the wide sidewalks

and wait for a flash

a vacuum or explosion

to rip my flesh with heat

and mingle my ashes with the city

No real idea of when

it might come

And so distraction eases

and the earth drops away

and I stumble back to the apartment

and I say hello and goodnight moon

and I return to comfort

and I begin to breathe

only until it pings my mind

again

How many seconds 'til midnight?

27.

Subway sway

on the toes and heels

the bodies in motion

close for a moment

then gone

Only a few eyes meet

enjoying the shared ride

the rest are fixed

on phones or books

or newspaper print

there's always something

between us

in a moment

to be placed in a pocket

perhaps you'll see me then

a flash of eyes

and gone

28.

Hope and fear

of being seen

I could write

and write and write

all the nothings

into somethings

empty days

like empty eyes

unmoved except for thought

endings becoming beginnings

filling time with body

words with rhythm

arriving in the moment

with changing conclusions

unable to tell

if chaos can be ordered

no matter

if the answer

cannot help

just another period

break or lift

pointing towards the unknown end.

29.

In the search for the most perfect phrasing

of the imperfect nature of the self

a grave error has been made

the adherence to structure

order, and theme

has overtaken the necessary expression

of the moment

and to be quite clear

the moment is/was the moment

and remains precisely where it is

the only hope for genuine articulation

must proceed from confession

and an unveiling of an attempt

to contain chaos

I do apologize

if at all you thought

my words made answers

of the unknown

You don't always need to know

the Truth

to recognize the presence of

the Lie.

30.

Write your hopes and fears in the corners of this page.

1) 2, 3, 5, 6, 10, 15, 30

2) (1)

3) (1), 4

4) (3), 6

5) (1), 6

6) (1, 4, 5), 10

7) 8, 9, 12

8) (7)

9) (7), 10

10) (1, 6, 9), 12

11) 12, 15, 20

12) (7, 10, 11)

13) 14, 15, 18

14) (13)

15) (1, 11, 13), 16

16) (15), 18, 20, 30

17) 18

18) (13, 16, 17)

19) 20, 21, 24

20) (11, 16, 19)

21) (19), 22, 25, 30

22) (21), 24

23) 24

24) (19, 22, 23)

25) (21), 26, 27, 30

26) (25), 30

27) (25), 28

28) (27), 30

29) 30

30) (1, 16, 21, 25, 26, 28, 29)

www.ingramcontent.com/pod-product-compliance
Lightning Source LLC
La Vergne TN
LVHW050931200726
843508LV00011B/2315